CONTEMPORARY LIVES

ADELE

GRAMMY-WINNING SINGER & SONGWRITER

ABDO
Publishing Company

CONTEMPORARY LIVES

ADELE

GRAMMY-WINNING SINGER & SONGWRITER

by Lisa Owings

CREDITS

Published by ABDO Publishing Company, PO Box 398166,
Minneapolis, MN 55439. Copyright © 2013 by Abdo Consulting
Group, Inc. International copyrights reserved in all countries.
No part of this book may be reproduced in any form without
written permission from the publisher. The Essential Library™ is a
trademark and logo of ABDO Publishing Company.

Printed in the United States of America,
North Mankato, Minnesota
112012
012013

 THIS BOOK CONTAINS AT LEAST 10% RECYCLED MATERIALS.

Editor: Rebecca Felix
Series Designer: Emily Love

Cataloging-in-Publication Data

Owings, Lisa.
 Adele: Grammy-winning singer & songwriter / Lisa Owings.
  p. cm. -- (Contemporary lives)
Includes bibliographical references and index.
ISBN 978-1-61783-616-9
1. Adele, 1988- --Juvenile literature. 2. Singers--England--
Biography--Juvenile literature. 1. Title.
782.42164092--dc15
[B]

2012945973

TABLE OF CONTENTS

At just 20 years old in 2008, Adele's powerful voice and relatable lyrics impressed both critics and fans.

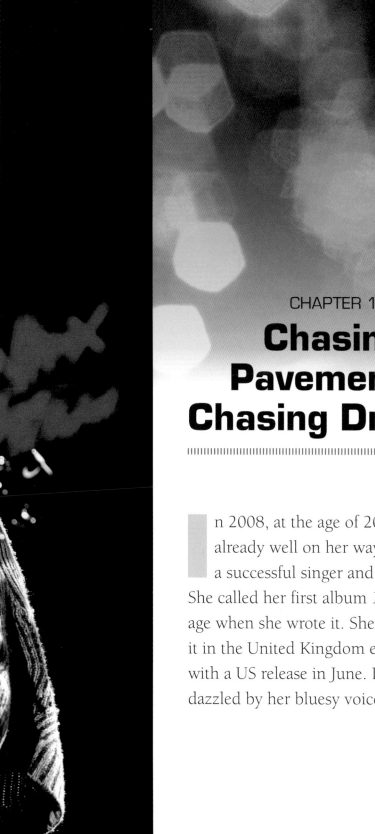

CHAPTER 1

Chasing Pavements, Chasing Dreams

‖‖‖

n 2008, at the age of 20, Adele was already well on her way to becoming a successful singer and songwriter. She called her first album *19*, after her age when she wrote it. She had released it in the United Kingdom early that year, with a US release in June. Listeners were dazzled by her bluesy voice and could relate to the stories of love and heartbreak she told through her songs.

People compared Adele to Amy Winehouse, a fellow British singer-songwriter. But one critic called Adele "simply too magical to compare her to anyone."[1] Reviewers described Adele's voice in many ways: sultry, soulful, funky, and dazzling.

On October 18, Adele was booked as the musical guest on the sketch comedy show *Saturday Night Live (SNL)* in New York City along with Alaska governor and 2008 vice presidential candidate Sarah Palin. Approximately 17 million people tuned in that night to see Palin. They were blindsided by Adele. She belted her songs "Chasing Pavements" and "Cold Shoulder" on the show, and after the performance, *19* rocketed to the top of the charts. Adele remembers this as the moment she realized she could make it big.

||||||||||||||||||||||||||||||||||||||||||||||||||||||||||||

ROAD TO THE GRAMMYS

Come December 2008, Adele was back home in London. Nominations for the upcoming Grammy Awards had just been announced. Adele sat in front of her computer, searching the Internet for news that fellow British singer-songwriter Leona Lewis had been nominated. Even if Adele felt she didn't stand a chance of being considered for such a prestigious award, she would be happy if a fellow Brit received the honor. In the midst of her search, Adele received an e-mail. She opened the message and was stunned by what it said: she had been nominated for a Grammy Award! Adele stared at the screen in shock as three more e-mails appeared in her inbox. She had been nominated for not just one, but four Grammy Awards: Best Female Pop Vocal Performance, Song of the Year, Record of the Year, and Best New Artist.

Adele was beside herself with excitement. But she didn't have much time to dwell on how surreal she felt at being nominated. She had to

> "I had to lock myself in the bathroom for an hour before I could come to terms with it. I couldn't believe it; it was a world where I never, ever thought I'd be included—not now or in the years to come."[2]
>
> —ADELE ON BEING NOMINATED FOR FOUR GRAMMY AWARDS IN 2009

prepare for an upcoming tour of North America in January 2009 and for the Grammy Awards in Los Angeles, California, that February.

To Adele's surprise, Anna Wintour, editor-in-chief of the fashion magazine *Vogue*, offered to be her stylist for the Grammys. Wintour helped the young singer create a look of timeless glamour. When Adele first tried on her romantic, full-skirted black dress accented with glittering diamonds, she felt ready to walk the red carpet with confidence. Yet as the night of the Grammy Awards crept closer, the singer's assuredness wavered.

At the last minute, Adele learned she would also be performing at the Grammys, which was a big honor. She would sing her hit single "Chasing Pavements" in front of a live audience of superstars as well as millions of television viewers. Adele loved singing live, but she suffered from severe, nausea-inducing stage fright before performances. Adding to her nerves, Adele was asked to perform at the MusiCares benefit concert in Los Angeles two nights before the awards ceremony. She agreed to do the MusiCares concert, but when she found out she would have to learn and perform a song

The chic ensemble *Vogue* editor Anna Wintour pulled together for Adele's Grammy Awards debut in 2009 gave the budding young star confidence.

she was unfamiliar with—"Cracklin' Rosie"—she panicked and nearly backed out.

It was all too much. Adele now had to prepare for two huge performances only days apart.

Her peers, idols, and millions of fans would be watching her. She was thousands of miles from her home, her family, and her friends. She wished she hadn't convinced her mother to stay behind in London. But somehow, Adele found the courage to go ahead with the MusiCares concert. And then it was on to the Grammys.

FIRST WIN

On the way to the awards ceremony on February 8, Adele's manager called to tell her she had already won her first Grammy. The winner for Best Female Pop Vocal Performance had been announced during the Grammy Awards pre-telecast. Adele, who had won for her

MUSICARES WITH NEIL DIAMOND

MusiCares is an organization dedicated to helping members of the music community with financial, medical, and personal needs. It also seeks to raise awareness of issues that threaten the welfare of the music industry. Neil Diamond was honored as the MusiCares Person of the Year in 2009. In paying tribute to Diamond, Adele was joined by singers Jennifer Hudson, Josh Groban, Tim McGraw, and the Jonas Brothers, in addition to many other star musicians.

single "Chasing Pavements," couldn't contain her excitement. She screamed at the top of her lungs. Then she remembered she had to sing later that night. She vowed the rest of her celebration would consist of drinking water out of a champagne glass.

With her first Grammy under her belt, Adele strolled down the red carpet. She posed for pictures and answered interview questions with charm and sincerity. As she waited to be ushered to her seat, Adele found herself standing with singer Neil Diamond and hip-hop artists P. Diddy and Jay-Z. When she sat down, other big-name celebrities, including rapper Snoop Dogg and the band U2, surrounded her. She felt so out of place she was afraid someone would ask her to leave. Adele was starstruck throughout the night as she interacted with fellow singers.

MORE SURPRISES

Adele felt certain one Grammy was all she could hope to win that night. She was so sure she wouldn't be accepting another award that by the time the presenters for Best New Artist stepped onstage, she had kicked off her shoes and popped a piece of chewing gum into her mouth. She hadn't even bothered to prepare a speech. Adele listened to the presenter, hip-hop artist Kanye West, list the nominees: her name, followed by Duffy, the Jonas Brothers, Lady Antebellum, and Jazmine Sullivan. After pausing to open the envelope, West pronounced the winner: "Adele!"[3]

Suddenly, strains of "Chasing Pavements" filled the auditorium. Adele's manager sent her down the aisle toward the stage. An emotional—and barefoot—Adele bounced up the stairs to the stage to accept her award. Clutching the award in her hands and nervously chomping her gum, she turned toward the microphone. "Thank you so much," she said. "I'm going to cry!"[4] Adele went on to thank her manager, mother, and record labels. She also expressed her admiration for fellow nominees Duffy and the Jonas Brothers. Then Adele hurried offstage to the sound of the crowd's enthusiastic cheers.

Shock and appreciation brought Adele close to tears as she accepted the Best New Artist award at the Grammys in 2009.

STAR PERFORMER

Adele had won two Grammy Awards, but she couldn't let loose and celebrate just yet. With a mixture of anxiety and excitement, she looked forward to her performance of "Chasing Pavements." If she was nervous as she took the stage again that night, it didn't show. The orchestra began to play and the lights dimmed as Adele

TOO SOON FOR A GRAMMY

Adele told the British Broadcasting Corporation (BBC) that winning a Grammy for her first album would be wonderful, but she felt it was an honor she didn't deserve just yet. She said,

> "I imagine it's like winning an Oscar, and I don't think on this record I should get one. I think it should be with my second or third record that I should get the Oscar, like from your third or fourth film when you're amazing."[5]

Adele also said she would be proud of her music even if she didn't win a Grammy Award. These statements got her in trouble in the United States, where people viewed her as ungrateful or dismissive of the Grammys. Adele later clarified her meaning, saying she just didn't want her career to peak with her first record.

eased into the first verse. When she got to the chorus, she unleashed the full power of her voice. Country singer Jennifer Nettles joined Adele onstage for the last part of the song. Their voices rose in harmony and then gradually faded. The audience burst into applause.

Adele had won two of the four Grammy Awards she was nominated for that night. When the glorious evening was over, Adele called her mother, who was so proud she burst into tears. Adele was happy and exhausted, but she patiently posed for

A gleeful Adele posed with her Grammy Awards after the show.

more photos—with a Grammy in each hand—and sat for a couple of brief interviews. Then she headed back to her hotel. She would fly home in the morning, where she could celebrate with her mother in person. "I don't see how my life could get any better," Adele said that night.[6]

||||||||||

Adele's childhood home in Tottenham, North London

104

CHAPTER 2

Adele
Laurie Blue

‖‖

Adele's mother, Penny Adkins, met Adele's father in 1987 at a pub in North London. Mark Evans was in his early twenties, and Adkins was 18. Evans fell in love with the teenage art student almost immediately, and the young couple soon moved in together. A few months later, they learned they were pregnant. Adkins and Evans welcomed their baby girl into the world on

May 5, 1988. Although Evans wanted "Blue" to be his daughter's first name ("after the music I love—the blues," he said) the couple settled on Adele Laurie Blue Adkins.[1] Evans took credit for exposing his daughter to the jazz, blues, and folk music that would later influence her style:

> I'd lie on the sofa all night, cradling Adele in my arms and listening to my favorite music—Ella Fitzgerald, Louis Armstrong, Bob Dylan, and Nina Simone. Night after night I'd play those records. I'm certain that is what shaped Adele's music.[2]

Evans also admitted that his daughter's brand of "heartbroken soul" was rooted in a difficult childhood from which he was largely absent.[3] He left Adkins when Adele was just a toddler. Adele saw her father only occasionally during her childhood. The two have never been close.

Left to raise her daughter on her own, Adkins struggled to make ends meet. She and Adele managed to scrape by living in Tottenham, a diverse district of North London riddled with crime and poverty. Adkins supplemented her meager artist's income by making furniture and

Growing up as the only child of a single mother, Adele's mom was her world. Adele knew Adkins chose to give up her own dreams so Adele's had a chance of coming true. The singer has never taken this for granted. Now that Adele is famous, she wants her mother to live the dream along with her. "Hopefully I'll sell 20 million records and she'll never have to work again," the star said.[5] To express her devotion, Adele even got a tattoo of a penny—her mother's namesake coin—on the inside of her wrist.

giving massages. Adele is intensely grateful for the sacrifices her mother made to give her a comfortable life, and despite the hardships, she remembers her childhood as a good one. "She's the most supportive mum ever. She's my best friend," Adele said.[4]

Adele's large extended family was instrumental in helping her grow into a happy-go-lucky child. She was especially close to her paternal grandfather, John Evans. Adele also enjoyed visiting her cousins, many of whom lived nearby. Both of Adele's parents later found love again, further expanding the family. Adkins began a long-term relationship with a man who Adele soon came to think of as a father. Evans had a child

Adele and her half-brother, Cameron, grew up apart and don't often see each other. Yet whenever they meet, they feel comfortable and immediately start teasing each other. Adele sees a lot of herself in Cameron. He looks almost exactly like her. He also has a similarly colorful personality. The only real difference between them, she says, is that she's more outgoing.

with his new girlfriend. Adele was thrilled with her half-brother, Cameron, whom she saw occasionally. Despite growing up in different homes, Adele and Cameron felt like true siblings.

BIG DREAMS

Adele did not grow up in a particularly musical household. Like many children, she enjoyed music and liked to sing along. Adele's parents encouraged her interest in singing and thought she had a lovely voice.

From around the age of three, Adele was fascinated by the shifting tones of people's voices. "I used to listen to how the tones would change from angry to excited to joyful to upset," she said.[6] At four, Adele was busily teaching herself to play a toy guitar. She also looked forward to Friday nights, when her mom let her stay up late to watch *Later . . . with Jools Holland*, a music program that featured famous artists and little-known ones.

By the age of five, Adele's musical tastes had developed to include a wide range of pop artists. She especially loved British acts the Spice Girls and Gabrielle. She also listened to US pop star Britney Spears and was fond of boy bands such as the Backstreet Boys and *NSYNC. Adkins loved to hear Adele sing her own versions of hit singles. In fact, she was so impressed by her daughter's talent she often had Adele give informal concerts to entertain company.

LATER . . . WITH JOOLS HOLLAND |||||||||||||||||||||||||

As Adele watched the BBC's *Later . . . with Jools Holland* each week with her mom, she had no idea she would one day be a guest on the show. Adele made her television debut on *Later . . . with Jools Holland* in June 2007.

She accompanied herself on acoustic guitar while singing "Daydreamer," a song that would later be released on *19*. She wrote "Daydreamer" about a friend she had fallen in love with and her romanticized daydreams about him.

Adele and her mother soon moved to Brixton, a rough area of South London, where Adele attended school with children of many different cultures and races. As she grew older, her friends introduced her to different kinds of music. Adele especially liked rhythm and blues (R&B), hip-hop, and soul music. By the time Adele was ten years old, music had become more than just her passion. It was her dream. "I [stole] my mum's Lauryn Hill album and listened to it every day after school . . . hoping to God that one day I'd be a singer," she recalled of that time in her life.[7]

THE BLUES

The year of 1999 brought heartbreak for 11-year-old Adele. Her beloved grandfather John died of cancer that year at the age of 57. Both Adele and her father were overcome with grief. The tragedy might have helped the two become closer, but instead of mourning with his daughter, Evans coped by drinking. His responsibilities as a father took a backseat to his alcoholism, and whatever bonds still existed between Adele and her father dissolved completely.

The music of singer-songwriter Lauryn Hill inspired Adele as she dreamed of becoming a performer.

Shortly after her grandfather's death, Adele moved to West Norwood—another area of South London—with her mom and stepfather. She enrolled in a new school, where her teachers seemed focused on squashing her potential and her friends seemed intent on growing up too fast. Adele's rebellious friends introduced her to grunge music and metal bands such as Slipknot and Korn. Adele loved the fashion associated with this scene—baggy jeans, hoodies, and dog collars—but she only pretended to like the music.

As Adele entered her early teens, her future seemed bleak. According to Adele, many of

A FATHER'S REGRETS

After a long estrangement with her father, Adele was almost ready to rebuild their relationship. However, in 2011 he betrayed her once again. Evans wanted his daughter's forgiveness, but instead of reaching out to Adele, he sold his story to the press. He told *The Sun*,

"I was not there for my daughter when I should have been, and I have regretted that every second of every day to this moment now. It tears me up inside."[8]

Adele was enraged when the story was published. She couldn't understand why her father would choose to sell a story rather than speak with her personally. "If I ever see him I will spit in his face," was her unforgiving response.[9]

her friends' ambitions were to become teenage
parents, and they weren't interested in getting jobs.
Adele wanted something more for herself, and
her mother was determined to help her achieve
her dreams.

||||||||||||

Although she was determined at an early age to pursue a singing career, Adele would be surprised by how soon her dream took shape.

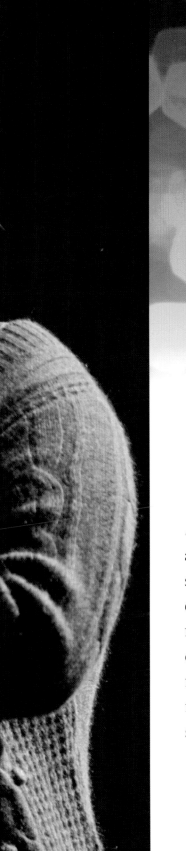

CHAPTER 3

Immersed in Music

||||||||||||||||||||||||||||||||||||||||||||||||

Adele's life changed course in 2002. At 14 years old, she knew she wanted to pursue a career in music. She decided to switch schools. Her mother was supportive and eager to help Adele find a high school to nurture her talents—and one that Adkins could afford. After considering a few more expensive options, Adele and her mother found the perfect performing arts school.

The BRIT School for Performing Arts & Technology lay just a short distance south of West Norwood in Croydon. BRIT stands for British Record Industry Trust. The trust supports the school's efforts to provide performance education and supplies the school with needed facilities. The school had a good reputation, having turned out such musical successes as singers Winehouse and Imogen Heap, as well as the band the Kooks. The school was also funded by the government, so Adkins wouldn't have to pay to send her daughter there. However, Adele would have to compete with numerous other budding musicians to enroll.

The young singer's audition interview went well: the BRIT School music director accepted her as a student. Her teachers encouraged her to pursue her own interests and artistic vision. All of Adele's classmates at the BRIT School seemed to want to make something of themselves. Adele flourished in this nurturing environment. In addition to singing lessons, she took courses in music production. She learned many practical skills that would serve her well later in life, including how to use recording equipment and decode legal contracts.

The BRIT School for Performing Arts & Technology in Croydon, London

FINDING HER VOICE

One day early in her BRIT School education, Adele bought some albums of jazz greats Etta James and Ella Fitzgerald. She said listening to those albums for the first time "changed [her] life."[1]

Adele learned more by listening to James and Fitzgerald than she ever did in her classes at school. The thing that struck her most about these artists was the passion and conviction in their voices. Adele was also impressed by the longevity

Jazz legend Etta James is Adele's favorite singer of all time. James was born in 1938. By the time she was 14, she was already in a band, the Peaches, and well on her way to fame. She released her first hit song, "The Wallflower," in 1954. James was signed to a record label in 1960, and her career took off throughout the late twentieth century. However, James's life was difficult and marred by drug use. The pain that came through in her voice is what made her music so believable for Adele. Adele was able to see her idol live in concert a couple of years before James passed away in January 2012 at the age of 73.

of these women's music, which had been made in the 1940s. Adele began to seek out other legendary musicians whose music had stood the test of time. She listened to jazz and R&B singer Roberta Flack, country and crossover star Johnny Cash, and the pop and soul group the Supremes. Adele longed to be the sort of singer people would still want to listen to 50 years down the road.

As Adele's musical tastes began to change, so did her voice. She picked up her soulful sound from James and her technical skill from Fitzgerald and Flack. Although these jazz legends were like singing coaches for Adele, she also learned a lot at the BRIT School. Her teachers helped her realize she could write her own music, a possibility that hadn't occurred to her before. It was only when she began writing her own songs that Adele found her true voice.

At 16, Adele wrote her first song, "Hometown Glory." As she sang about her experiences and feelings about living in London, sincerity and passion naturally came through in her voice. Adele realized that writing what she knew and singing from the heart was the key to making people believe in her music. This was also the age when Adele learned to play the guitar. The ability to play music to accompany her singing gave her acoustic performances an air of intimacy and simplicity.

NEW FRIENDS

The BRIT School fostered a collaborative environment in which students helped one another grow. Among Adele's classmates was singer Shingai Shoniwa, who inspired Adele greatly. The charismatic rock musician and her family moved next door to Adele and her family, and Shoniwa

SHINGAI SHONIWA

Adele's West Norwood neighbor, Shingai Shoniwa, also found fame thanks to the BRIT School. She started a band with classmates Dan Smith and Jamie Morrison. They called themselves the Noisettes, with Shoniwa as the lead vocalist. Shoniwa attracted critics' attention with her magical voice and her wild fashions. A critic called the singer "a living, breathing manifestation of the rock & roll spirit."[2]

attended school with Adele. The two soon started jamming together. As their friendship grew, they found they had much in common. Like Adele, Shoniwa had been raised in South London by her mother. Her father died when she was 11 years old. Their past struggles gave both singers an edge of soulfulness, and their jam sessions helped Adele develop a more mature sound.

Following "Hometown Glory," Adele wrote two more songs: "Daydreamer" and "My Same." She recorded demos of the songs for a class project, but she didn't know how to use them to promote her music. One of Adele's more Internet-savvy friends posted the demos on MySpace, a social networking site, where they soon caught the attention of the world outside of the BRIT School.

||||||||||

Just as her neighbor and schoolmate Adele did, singer Shingai Shoniwa went on to perform professionally.

In the years following high school, Adele's music career took off and her life changed dramatically.

CHAPTER 4

19

|||||||||||||||

Between 2004 and 2006, while Adele was finishing up her last two years at the BRIT School, her demo tracks were growing more popular on MySpace every day. But Adele paid no attention to the MySpace page her friend had set up for her. Even when the friend told Adele she was receiving messages from important players in the music industry, Adele dismissed the idea as impossible.

The day Adele finished high school in May 2006, her friend gave her the password to the MySpace page. He encouraged her to log in and respond to the messages she had been getting, which he suspected were serious offers. Adele followed his advice. Three days later, the incredulous 18-year-old met with the executives of record label XL Recordings. Although the label didn't sign Adele right away, they were impressed by her maturity and her strong sense of who she was as an artist.

XL RECORDINGS

Record labels such as XL Recordings—the record label that signed Adele—help an artist produce, manufacture, distribute, and market albums. In return, the label receives a share of the artist's profits. This deal is arranged when the artist signs a contract with the company. The London-based record label XL Recordings was founded in 1989. Over the next couple of decades, its reputation grew as large as its name. Adele joined groundbreaking XL artists including electronic music group the Prodigy, singer-songwriter Beck, singer-songwriter-rapper M.I.A, and rock bands the White Stripes, Radiohead, and Vampire Weekend.

LIFE ON THE LABEL

In June, XL Recordings introduced Adele to Jonathan Dickins, head of September Management. The two hit it off, and Dickins agreed to become Adele's manager. Dickins and Adele began working together right away, and by the end of September that year Dickins got Adele a recording contract with XL Recordings.

The singer was in awe that she had landed a record deal just months after graduating from high school. However, it would be quite some time before she felt up to the task of producing an album. At the moment, Adele just wanted to have fun. She spent the next several months hanging out with friends, staying up late, and watching the television show *Sex and the City*.

Adele also discovered her love of performing live during this time. In December 2006, she opened for her friend and fellow XL artist Jack Peñate at an intimate venue called the Troubadour in London. The place was packed and uncomfortably hot. But the atmosphere changed when Adele released her first bluesy notes into the air. The crowd fell silent. Adele's singing commanded their full attention. As Adele scanned the audience, she noticed some people's faces were streaked with tears. She was touched that her music could evoke such an emotional response. In a later interview, Adele said she remembered thinking, "'Oh my God, this is amazing. [I] can't live without it.'" She added, "There's nothing more freeing than playing live, nothing."[1]

Throughout early 2007, Adele continued playing at small venues in London and touring with other musicians around the United Kingdom. She knew she was supposed to be writing more songs for her first album, but she just didn't feel inspired. Besides, she was busy performing and having fun.

||||||||||||||||||||||||||||||||||||||||||||||||||||||

HEARTBROKEN

Adele got a jolt of inspiration soon enough. She found out her boyfriend at the time had cheated on her. Adele tracked him down at a London pub and confronted him about it. Then she punched him in the face. When security threatened to throw her out of the pub, she ran. The pub security chased Adele down busy Oxford Street for a while

Adele enjoyed playing live,
although it made her nervous.

before giving up. "And then I just kept running," she recalled, "even though they weren't chasing me anymore. I was running *from* something. And I didn't know what. I was just chasing a pavement."[2] Even in the midst of her anguish, Adele registered the lyricism of the phrase. As soon as she got home, she wrote the hit song "Chasing Pavements," which later earned Adele her first Grammy Award.

The rest of the songs that would appear on her debut album, *19*, poured out over the course of three weeks in May 2007. All of them were inspired by Adele's recent heartbreak. She wrote the songs as part of her own healing process, not thinking about the millions of people who would soon be listening to her most private feelings.

|||||||||||||||||||||||||||||||||||||||||||||||||||||||||||

ACCOMPLISHED ARTIST

That June, Adele was a guest on *Later . . . with Jools Holland*. It was her first television appearance in the United Kingdom. As her album was still in the works, she performed "Daydreamer," one of the three songs she had written prior to landing her record deal. The song became popular on the radio late that year.

Over the next few months, Adele and her producers worked to put the finishing touches on *19*. But it was her manager, Dickins, whose input made the album feel complete. Adele had already recorded what she thought would be the last song on *19* when Dickins played her "Make You Feel My Love" by US singer-songwriter Bob Dylan. It was one of the most beautiful songs Adele had ever heard. She felt the lyrics said everything she had been trying to convey on the album. Adele made room on the album for her heartbreaking rendition of the song. The last-minute addition brought a

"MAKE YOU FEEL MY LOVE"

Celebrated folk musician Bob Dylan wrote "Make You Feel My Love" for his forty-first album, *Time Out of Mind*, in 1997. Although the song received mixed reviews at the time of its release, other artists boosted its popularity. Among many others, singer-songwriter Billy Joel and country singer Garth Brooks covered the ballad, both to much success. Adele's cover of the song was also popular. British newspaper the *Guardian* said of her version, "[Adele] summons a passion that its croaking author could only envy."[3]

sense of wholeness and closure to the album. Adele knew it was finished.

The first single from *19*, "Hometown Glory," was released in October 2007. Even though she had only released one single, Adele gained enough popularity to headline during a tour of the United Kingdom. Many of the shows were sold out. As before, Adele performed at intimate venues that allowed her to really connect with her audience. Now that she had more stage time as the main act, she started telling stories between songs. She sprinkled in charming jokes, liberal profanity, and startlingly loud bursts of laughter before launching into another song. Audiences couldn't get enough of Adele. They eagerly anticipated the release of *19*, which was scheduled for January.

In December, Adele revealed her second single from the album. She performed "Chasing Pavements" for the first time on television during British comedy show *Friday Night with Jonathan Ross*. The single was officially released in mid-January. Also in December, Adele became the first-ever winner of the Critic's Choice Award, the newest category of BRIT Awards. It meant approximately 1,000 music critics had predicted

Adele at the Brit Awards in 2008, where she won the Critic's Choice Award

After musicians are finished recording and producing an album, they need to market that album in order for its release to be successful. Like Adele, many artists embark on promotional tours to build anticipation. They often appear on television and radio shows or perform concerts to raise awareness about their music. Releasing singles before unveiling the whole album is another way artists get people excited about their music. This way, when the album is finally released, it is more likely to sell well.

hers would be the most successful debut album released in 2008.

||||||||||||||||||||||||||||||||||||||||||||||||||||||||

DAZZLING DEBUT

In late January 2008, Adele unleashed her debut album on the United Kingdom. Its 12 tracks included "Melt My Heart to Stone," Adele's favorite, as well as future hits "Cold Shoulder" and "Right as Rain." *19* instantly became the Number 1 album in the country. Her single "Chasing Pavements" shot to Number 2 on the charts.

While some critics thought *19* didn't live up to the hype, most gave the record glowing reviews.

The *Guardian* praised Adele's "wonderful soulful phrasing, the sheer unadulterated pleasure of her voice" and called her "a rare singer."[4] After rushing out to purchase the album, Adele's fans heartily agreed.

||||||||||||

By 2008, British fans were in awe of Adele's talent, and she was ready to make her US debut.

CHAPTER 5

Adele in America

||||||||||||||||||||||||||||||||||||||||||||||||

H aving dazzled the United Kingdom with her first album, Adele felt ready to take on North America. She got her opportunity in March 2008. XL Recordings teamed with US label Columbia Records to release *19* in the United States that summer.

Adele was surprised at the enthusiasm her music had garnered internationally, and she was eager to show her fans how grateful she was for their support. That month, Adele set off on a brief tour of North America. By late April, she was back in the United Kingdom. The singer played several concerts in her native country before returning to North America to tour again.

|||||||||||||||||||||||||||||||||||||||||||||||||||||||||||||

AN EVENING WITH ADELE

Adele embarked on her concert tour An Evening with Adele in May. Her debut album was scheduled to be released in the United States in June. Adele had a pared-down touring style that made her stand out from other famous pop artists. Instead of performing in outrageous costumes and using dancers and pyrotechnics to entertain her audience, Adele kept her shows focused on what she did best: music. Accompanied by a small band, or sometimes just her guitar, Adele's vocals made a big statement—possibly more so than other popular singers' shocking wardrobes or extravagant props. "I love seeing Lady Gaga . . . . I love seeing Katy Perry. . . . But that's not what my music is about," Adele later explained. "I don't make music for eyes. I make music for ears."[1]

For the most part, being on tour was a high for Adele. Although there were low points too, she described touring as "better than making a record or winning awards. I love just going and playing to real people."[2] In addition to touring, Adele promoted her album by doing radio and television interviews and performances, which helped her reach an even wider audience.

19's US RELEASE

19 was released in the United States on June 10, 2008, in the midst of one of the North American legs of An Evening with Adele. As it had in the United Kingdom, Adele's debut album wowed US critics.

Although comparisons between Adele and fellow British singer Winehouse were common

19 CERTIFIED PLATINUM

By March 2008, Adele's first album was already certified platinum in the United Kingdom, which meant more than 300,000 copies of 19 had been sold in that country. In March 2011, three years and hundreds of thousands of sales later, 19 was certified quadruple platinum in the United Kingdom.

US critics praised Adele's dynamic vocals and heartfelt songwriting.

in the United States, most reviewers dismissed them. They gave Adele credit for cultivating her own unique sound on *19*. Many critics knew the already-stunning Adele would continue growing musically. *Billboard* prophetically stated, "Adele truly has potential to become among the most respected and inspiring international artists of her generation."[3]

HOMESICK AND LOVESICK

Despite her warm welcome in North America, Adele soon began to miss home. Each performance was more emotionally draining than the last. Although she enjoyed singing live, Adele was physically ill with stage fright before every show. At times she felt she was reliving her heartbreak through every song. Eventually, the 20-year-old found herself longing to be back in London among family and friends. She drank and smoked cigarettes to cope. Even if alcohol helped take her mind off home, it couldn't tear Adele's thoughts away from the person she missed most—a man she had secretly fallen in love with that summer.

By the fall of 2008, Adele had decided she couldn't bear to be away from her secret love. After appearing on a few US television shows in early September, she canceled several concert dates and

SINGING SOBER

After Adele's alcohol consumption led to problems on her US tour, the singer decided to quit drinking. She soon realized how important the decision was for her career. "I'm quite enjoying [being sober]," she said. "I can remember everything that I do!"[4] Adele began making a point of not drinking while she is working.

cited personal problems as an excuse to return to London. She later admitted she had backed out of her commitments and disappointed her fans in order to spend more time with her secret boyfriend. She acknowledged the move as "ungrateful" and noted that her heavy drinking at the time had clouded her judgment.[5] Still, Adele didn't completely regret her time out of the international spotlight.

RISING FAME

In October, Adele returned to the United States. One of the producers for *SNL* had discovered Adele

MYSTERY MAN

Fans have come to know a lot about the man Adele began dating in the summer of 2008. Incredibly, however, Adele managed to keep his identity under wraps. Tabloids published rumored romances with actor and musician Slinky Winfield, DJ Ned Biggs, and fashion photographer Alex Sturrock. Whoever Adele canceled her tour dates for, it seems he was a bad influence. "[Drinking] was kind of the basis of my relationship with this boy," she later admitted.[6] Even so, Adele gives him credit for changing her life and bringing her across the threshold of adulthood. "If I hadn't met him," she said, "I'd still be that little girl I was when I was eighteen."[7]

at a show in New York. He offered her a spot as a musical guest on the show on October 18, and she jumped at the opportunity.

Adele appeared on the *SNL* stage in her signature look: a dark ensemble complemented by a backcombed ponytail and false eyelashes. She performed her two songs flawlessly, and her humility as she stepped away from the microphone endeared her to her audience. Her *SNL* appearance entranced the millions of people watching and snagged the attention of Grammy voters. Literally overnight, Adele became a star in the United States.

November found Adele back in London, where she moved out of her mother's home and into a place of her very own. She bought her first apartment in Notting Hill, a posh area of London with a thriving artistic community. Adele had a few weeks to settle in before she had to be back on the road. It all seemed so surreal. At 20, she was enjoying international success, a glamorous new apartment, and a blossoming romance.

In a continued upswing, Adele found out in December she was nominated for four Grammy Awards. She was also asked to sing "Chasing

Adele performing at the
Grammy Awards in 2009

Pavements" during the awards ceremony. At the Grammys on February 8, 2009, Adele proved to the world she belonged in the ranks of musical superstars—even if she didn't believe it herself. Her Grammy performance was worthy of the two awards she took home that night, including Best New Artist. The Grammy wins were just the thing to help Adele get through the final months of her lengthy tour.

||||||||||

Amid her busy schedule of performances in 2009, Adele also began putting thought into a new album.

CHAPTER 6

21

IIIIIIIIIIIIIIII

Just two days after the 2009 Grammy Awards, Adele received another pleasant surprise. Her agent had asked Adele's musical idol, Etta James, to coheadline a concert with Adele that June at the Hollywood Bowl amphitheater in Los Angeles, California. The 71-year-old jazz diva agreed. Adele couldn't wait to meet James. She predicted the concert with James would be "the best night ever."[1] However, she still had several months of touring to get through before then.

On short breaks Adele took between portions of her tour, she began thinking about her next album. She was in no real hurry and wanted to take the time to produce an album that would be even more successful than 19. As had happened the first time, it took Adele a while to find inspiration. She knew for her second album to do well, she needed to write songs other people could relate to. She also knew she needed to draw from her own life in order to sing with the passion she had expressed on 19. Yet Adele's life over the past year had been all but disconnected from the lives of average people. She decided she had to wait until she had lived through another universal human experience.

IIIIIIIIIIIIIIIIIIIIIIIIIIIIIIIIIIIIIIIIIIIIIIIIIIIIIIIIIIIIII

OUT OF LOVE

Unfortunately for Adele—but fortunately for her music—that experience came in the spring of 2009. Adele's romance with her beau grew stale and slowly fizzled out. She said of the breakup,

This time, nobody did anything wrong. We just fell out of love with one another and I had to deal with the devastation of feeling like a failure because I couldn't make things work.[2]

In many ways, this breakup was more painful than the one that had inspired *19* because there was nothing concrete to blame it on. Songwriting again helped Adele move on.

By May 2009, Adele had drafted the first few songs for her next album. Although a couple of them were upbeat, the rest of the songs dealt with the sadness and regret of lost love. On May 5, in the midst of writing through her relationship woes, Adele celebrated her twenty-first birthday far away from home.

BIRTHDAY GIRL

On May 5, 2009, Adele played a show in New York City. It was her twenty-first birthday and she was disappointed she couldn't be with her family. She had no idea her family had come to her in New York until her mother surprised her onstage with a towering birthday cake and balloons. Adele was overjoyed to see her mom. Afterward, the singer attended a small party with her band. She called it a night early because she wanted to be fresh for her appearance on the television show *MTV Unplugged* the next day.

UGLY BETTY, BEAUTIFUL STARS

Adele was good at acting calm during performances, hiding the anxiety and sadness she often felt onstage. An opportunity to showcase these acting skills came about when the producers of the television show *Ugly Betty*, which was filmed in New York City, asked her to do a cameo appearance. Adele was excited to make her acting debut alongside *Ugly Betty* star America Ferrera, whom the singer had met in her dressing room at *SNL* the previous October. On the episode titled "In the Stars," which aired on May 14, Adele played herself meeting one of her fans (Betty), and then she sang her song "Right as Rain."

It seemed fitting for Adele and Ferrera to appear on television together. Both stars were seen as important role models for women, especially curvy women. Both had declared war on the impractical stick-thin standard of beauty that held sway in the entertainment industry. Adele was confident in how she looked. She had already proved she didn't need to be thin or flaunt her body to be successful. In fact, the singer felt as though looking more like the average woman than a fashion model was an

Seeing her idol Etta James in concert was an emotional experience for Adele.

advantage. "Fans are encouraged that I'm not a size zero," she said.[3] In another interview, she explained how her appearance and performance style helped people take her seriously as a musician. "I don't want people confusing what it is that I'm about," she said.[4]

HOLLYWOOD BOWL

Adele had some time off in May between filming *Ugly Betty* and her upcoming Hollywood Bowl concert with James, but she didn't fly home right away. She stayed in New York to attend one of James's concerts, and a nervous Adele met the singer for the first time backstage afterward. Adele returned to London in mid-May. It would be another month and a half before she took the stage with James in Los Angeles. In the meantime, Adele decompressed by spending time in the studio.

> "I cried as soon as I sat down. [Etta James] was phenomenal. I closed my eyes on 'Sugar on the Floor' and 'At Last,' and it was like I was there back in the day. She was so funny and witty and raunchy and sarcastic and cheeky, and her voice . . . [was] so amazing!"[5]
>
> —ADELE ON SEEING ETTA JAMES PERFORM

As the date for the Hollywood Bowl concert approached, Adele grew more and more excited. Coheadlining with James was a dream come true. The show would also mark the end of Adele's US tour. With the exception of one last tour performance in the Netherlands in July, Adele would be free to focus on her second album. She couldn't wait.

But things didn't quite go as planned. James was forced to cancel her Hollywood Bowl appearance at the last minute due to illness. Adele was crushed, but she wasn't about to disappoint the 17,000 fans that would fill the arena on June 28. She headlined the sold-out show, and legendary funk-R&B singer-songwriter Chaka Khan took James's place. Adele was so in awe of the enormous crowd that night she forgot some of her lyrics. Onstage, Adele joked about her forgetfulness, and the crowd was happy to forgive her. All in all, the night was a success.

A BUSY BREAK, THEN BACK TO WORK

Adele flew home from Los Angeles in early July 2009. After a bit of relaxation, the singer quickly filled her schedule. She met with her producer about her second album, performed the last show of her tour at the North Sea Jazz Festival in the Netherlands, took driving lessons, went to a few concerts, and made plans to get a dog.

In August, Adele vacationed in sunny Portugal with her friends, but it was hard to keep her thoughts from drifting back to her failed relationship. She took comfort in the fact that her broken heart would be helpful in writing her next album. Shortly after Adele returned from Portugal, she brought a new companion into her life: a dachshund puppy she named after jazz trumpet player Louis Armstrong.

After several weeks of relaxation, it was time for Adele to finally buckle down and work on her second album. She lost herself in analyzing other people's music for a while before getting back into a songwriting groove. She hoped her discoveries would help improve her writing.

In October, Adele teamed up with well-known British producer Paul Epworth to finish writing the song "Rolling in the Deep," which would become the biggest hit on her album. They recorded a demo of the song that day and ended up using the

MOVING IN WITH MUM |||||||||||||||||||||||||||||||||||||||||||||||||||||||||

As Adele settled into the more relaxed pace of everyday life in London after her tour, she realized her puppy Louis's company wasn't enough. She missed her mother. "I couldn't really function without her," she said.[6] So in October 2009, the star bought a large apartment in Battersea, South London, where she and her mother could live together.

original vocal track on the final album. Epworth said of the decision to keep Adele's first take,

> She had had her heart broken . . . and you can really hear that, her anger and her sadness. Sometimes I just don't think you can recreate that or fake it.[7]

MAKING 21

Adele's second album, *21*, was much more of a collaborative effort than *19* had been. In addition to Epworth and XL in London, Adele also worked with influential US producer Rick Rubin, copresident of Columbia Records. She cowrote many of the songs on the album with professional songwriters she admired. Adele felt the guidance of these accomplished producers and songwriters helped her grow as an artist and achieve a different sound—one that projected more attitude than her first album.

Adele's extensive travels also influenced her sound. While touring in the United States, Adele had been introduced to country, bluegrass, rockabilly, and gospel music. These American genres appealed to her for the same reason classic jazz had: they felt honest. Adele drew inspiration from these genres as she shaped 21.

Rubin, the main producer for 21, wanted to give Adele and her collaborators time to brainstorm, record, tweak, and rerecord until they had come up with something extraordinary. By early 2010, Adele had recorded a few songs in various studios around London. Rubin invited her to finish the album at the infamous Shangri-La Studio in Malibu, California, where the creativity of the band Metallica, singers Bonnie Raitt and Eric Clapton, and many other musicians had been nurtured. In April, she arrived in Malibu ready to record.

The Shangri-La experience was a slice of paradise. Adele was allowed to follow her instincts, and the production team quickly realized they had a prodigy on their hands. Adele could record a song perfectly in one take. Instead of mixing the vocal track with a prerecorded background, Adele sang with her musicians live in the studio. The result was magical. The recordings sounded as fresh and raw as live performances.

Adele injects passion into her songs each time she sings them, a practice leading her to record some songs on *21* in a single take.

> "The entire vocal [track] took about ten minutes [to record]. [Adele] sang it once top to bottom, pitch perfect; she didn't miss a note. I looked at the [sound] engineer, then at her and said, 'Adele, I don't know what to tell you but I have never had anyone do that in ten years.' Putting a vocal [track] on typically takes around four or five hours to make perfect; she did it in one take."[8]
>
> —PRODUCER AND SONGWRITER RYAN TEDDER ON RECORDING "RUMOR HAS IT"

"SOMEONE LIKE YOU"

In the midst of producing 21, Adele received a text saying her recent ex had gotten engaged. The fact that he became so serious with someone else so soon after their breakup was a huge blow. To deal with the pain, she wrote a song. Adele took the draft of "Someone Like You" to singer-songwriter Dan Wilson, who composed a simple piano melody to complement her heartfelt words.

"Someone Like You" earned the last slot on Adele's second album. It completed the range of emotions Adele had worked through on 21—from wanting revenge on her ex, to remembering the good times, to wanting him back, to letting him go. By the end of October 2010, the record was complete. Adele announced the official album title in early November. The first single, "Rolling in the Deep," was released later that month. However, fans would have to wait until early 2011 to hear the rest of the album.

||||||||||

Adele performed promoting her album *21* in 2011.

CHAPTER 7

Adele Live

||||||||||||||||||||||||||||||||||||||||||||||||||||||||||||||||

After making a few promotional appearances in December 2010 and January 2011, Adele was excited to release *21* on January 24 in Europe. Most of the continent clamored to hear it. The foot-stomping "Rolling in the Deep" and heart-wrenching "Someone Like You" are accompanied by other spectacular tracks on the album, including the infectious "Rumor Has It" and powerful "Set Fire to the Rain."

The breadth of musical influences and depth of writing on the album combined with Adele's vocals almost universally impressed critics. A BBC review praised 21 as "so marvelous, you're almost compelled to stand up and applaud it after the first listen."[1] "Someone Like You" stood out as particularly breathtaking. The *Guardian* said the song was "nearly good enough reason to break up with someone, simply so you can mope in it."[2]

The extra two years of experience Adele had gained as a woman and as a musician showed in the differences between her first and second albums. *19* had been a success, but *21* resonated with people in a way her first record hadn't. European fans went crazy for *21*, buying more than 200,000 copies in the first week after its release and sending it straight to the top of the UK albums chart. At the same time, *19* rose to the Number 4 spot, making Adele one of the very few artists to have two of her albums share the top five. That January was just the beginning of what would be a wildly successful year for Adele.

ADELE FEVER

February proved even busier for Adele. On February 15, she gave a shattering performance of "Someone Like You" at the BRIT Awards in London. By the end of the song, she was so overcome with emotion that her voice was shaking, and the audience was on their feet.

"I was really emotional by the end because I'm quite overwhelmed by everything anyway, and then I had a vision of my ex—of him watching me at home and he's going to be laughing at me because he knows I'm crying because of him, with him thinking, 'Yep, she's still wrapped around my finger.' Then everyone stood up, so I was overwhelmed."[3]

—ADELE ON PERFORMING "SOMEONE LIKE YOU" AT THE 2011 BRIT AWARDS

"Someone Like You" leapt from Number 47 to Number 1 on the UK charts, joining "Rolling in the Deep" in the top five. *21* was going into its fourth week at Number 1, and Adele became the first artist since iconic British pop band the Beatles in 1964 to see two of her albums and two of her singles make the top five on the UK charts at once.

Meanwhile, the upcoming US release of *21* was approaching. Columbia Records decided to get Adele as much exposure as possible—especially on television—to promote her album. Adele blazed through the talk show circuit, appearing on popular television shows *The Today Show*, *David Letterman*, *The Ellen Degeneres Show*, *Jimmy Kimmel Live*, and *The Early Show* over a span of ten days surrounding *21*'s February 22 release. The album burned up the US charts in its first week, debuting at Number 1 with a staggering 352,000 sales.

ON THE ROAD AGAIN

In March, Adele embarked on her world tour Adele Live. For this tour, Adele had a special stipulation in her tour rider, which is a list of requests set by an artist that must be met in order for them to perform. She mandated that any person who received a free ticket for her concert, whether through a promotion or from herself or venue staff, must donate to a charity of Adele's choice. Adele chose Sands, a charity in the United Kingdom that supports research on infant death prevention and provides counseling to those affected by it. Adele's

For her Adele Live concert, the singer's minimal stage effects included dim lamps and glowing lights.

nonnegotiable term was that a minimum amount of $20 was donated for each ticket received for free. Adele spent the first month touring Europe, playing in a different major city at least every other night. Every show was sold out. The total amount raised for Sands from the European leg of the tour was $13,000.

The singer stuck to her simple performing style for Adele Live. A few special lighting effects were the only visual distractions. Adele's vocals were supported by a five-piece band and a couple of backup singers. The sincerity of Adele's singing and her candid chatter made even the largest venues feel intimate.

Adele had a short break before traveling to North America for the second leg of her tour. Concerts had been scheduled in the United States and Canada throughout May and June. Approximately ten performances in, Adele's voice was suddenly reduced to a hoarse whisper. She panicked. There was no way she could sing that night. But by the next day, Adele convinced herself she could make it through one more show. While she was singing, she felt something rip in her throat. Doctors diagnosed it as a vocal hemorrhage—Adele had pushed her voice so hard her vocal cords bled. She was forced to cancel the rest of her US tour or risk permanent damage to her voice. She rescheduled the concerts so as not to disappoint her fans, and then she allowed herself a month's rest before reappearing onstage in London.

After two London performances in July—as well as nominations for a Mercury Prize and multiple Video Music Awards (VMAs)—Adele headed back to North America in August. She made it through all of her rescheduled performances, finishing out her time in the United States performing at the VMAs and collecting multiple awards. Adele's voice showed little sign of strain from the intense schedule. But by the beginning of September, when she was back in the United Kingdom for the next leg of her tour, her body had rebelled. A bad chest cold set in. Adele once again had to cancel several performances.

Approximately two weeks later, Adele had recovered enough to continue her UK tour. She sang in venues across England and Scotland. A concert in the famed Royal Albert Hall in London was especially thrilling. Adele's performance, which was filmed to be released on DVD, went beautifully, pairing her powerful songs with touches of her

ROYAL ALBERT HALL

The Royal Albert Hall in Westminster, London, was built between 1867 and 1871 as a memorial to Prince Albert, the husband of Queen Victoria, who ruled from 1837 until her death in 1901. Today, the hall continues to be a prestigious venue for concerts, balls, and other events.

The DVD of Adele's performance there, *Adele: Live at Royal Albert Hall*, shows the artist in her element. It captures her soaring vocals and comedic banter, alternating wide shots of the dramatic hall with close-ups of Adele and the other musicians.

candid humor. The concert would be one of her last before everything went wrong.

|||||||||||||||||||||||||||||||||||||||||||||||||||||||

ADELE SILENCED

At the start of October, Adele was gearing up for the final leg of her Adele Live tour. She would soon be back in the United States for a series of ten concerts. In the meantime, the singer had opened her heart to another man. She and Simon Konecki, head of the charity Drop4Drop, which aids the global water crisis, began dating that month. Adele was in love and happier than ever when she lost her voice again. It was another vocal hemorrhage. This time, a month's rest wouldn't be enough to heal it. Adele was devastated to have to cancel the entire last leg of her tour.

Adele's team sent her to a renowned US throat surgeon who examined the singer's throat and found she had developed a polyp, or growth of tissue, on her vocal cords. Adele was terrified to learn the growth would need to be surgically removed in order to restore her voice. If one wrong move was made during the surgery, Adele's career

Adele and Simon Konecki in February 2012, a little more than a year after they began dating

Adele's recovery would have been a lot more difficult if she hadn't had her beau, Simon Konecki, by her side. Konecki is 13 years Adele's senior. His charity, Drop4Drop, helps provide developing nations with clean, drinkable water. Contrary to rumors he was married when he started dating Adele, Konecki was long divorced. "He's wonderful," Adele said of her sweetheart. "And he's proud of me, but he doesn't care about what I do or what other people think. He looks after me."[4] Just as Konecki is supportive of Adele's career, she supports his charity. On clean water day, March 22, 2012, Adele took to Twitter to urge people to get involved with and become informed about Drop4Drop.

could be over. But Adele trusted her surgeon, and the operation was scheduled for November 3.

The surgery went well. Then came the hard part: recovery. The notoriously chatty Adele had to spend much of the rest of November in complete silence. The silence ended up being just what she needed. It gave her time to heal—both physically and emotionally—from the strain of leading such a fast-paced life.

GETTING READY FOR THE GRAMMYS

At the end of November, Adele had to fight the urge to scream when she found out she had been nominated for a whopping six Grammy Awards: Record of the Year, Song of the Year, Album of the Year, Best Pop Solo Performance, Best Pop Vocal Album, and Best Short Form Music Video. Careful not to strain her voice, Adele expressed her joy through a flood of tears.

Joy soon turned to a mixture of excitement and panic when Adele was invited to perform at the Grammy Awards in February 2012. She had slowly been building her voice back up throughout December. By the end of 2011, she was singing again. To Adele's delight, it felt smoother than ever to sing. Adele was confident her Grammy performance would not disappoint her audience. Still, she knew the millions of people watching the awards would be carefully scrutinizing every note—which was enough to make any performer nervous.

||||||||||

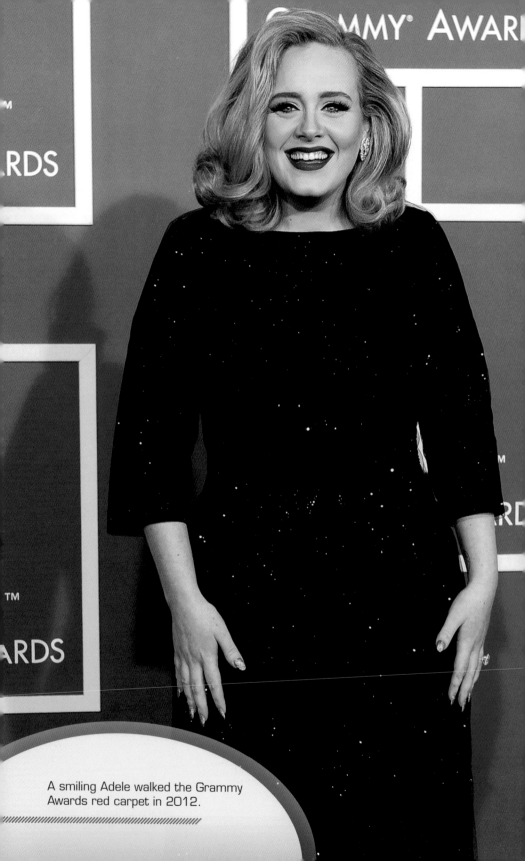

A smiling Adele walked the Grammy Awards red carpet in 2012.

CHAPTER 8
Right as Rain

||||||||||||||||||||||||||||||||||||||||||||||||||||||||||||||||||||||||||||||||||||||||||||

A dele arrived on the red carpet at the Grammy Awards the evening of February 12, 2012, sparkling in a black Giorgio Armani gown that hugged her figure, which touring and post-surgery dietary restrictions had slimmed. The singer had gone blonde, red lips framed her smile, and her signature long lashes fringed her eyes. Adele no longer felt out of place at the Grammy Awards—her name was on everyone's lips that night.

At the same time, singer Whitney Houston's tragic passing the day before weighed heavily on people's minds. A record television audience of nearly 40 million viewers tuned in to watch the Grammys, anticipating tributes to the iconic Houston. They were also anxiously awaiting Adele's first public performance since her surgery. Most of the viewers, artists, and critics watching believed Adele could win all six awards for which she had been nominated.

GRAMMY QUEEN

Before Adele snuggled into her seat next to boyfriend Konecki, she had already won her first two Grammys of the night. Her wins for Best Short Form Music Video and Best Pop Vocal Album had been announced during the pre-telecast ceremony while most stars had still been strolling the red carpet. Less than a half hour after the ceremony began, Adele took the stage to accept the Best Pop Solo Performance award for "Someone Like You." With gum in her mouth but her heels still on, Adele thanked the cowriter of the song she said had changed her life, as well as the doctors who healed her voice. By the time she accepted the Song of the Year award for "Rolling in the Deep," Adele had changed her dress for her performance later that evening. It was black and lacy with polka-dotted mesh sweeping up her neck and down her arms. The singer, chuckling and chomping her gum, said a quick thank-you before offering cowriter and producer Epworth the microphone.

Finally, it was time for Adele to perform. Adele's voice surged through the dark auditorium as she sang the first few bars of the "Rolling in the Deep" chorus a cappella. The strength and clarity of her voice washed over the audience, and she began the first verse. Everyone clapped in time as Adele belted her hit with more attitude than ever. Adele couldn't hold back a triumphant cackle at the end, likely overjoyed in defying those who thought she

SALES SPIKE

After the 2012 Grammy Awards, Adele experienced yet another surge in sales of the wildly popular *21*. Fans purchased 730,000 copies of the album in the week following the ceremony, an increase of nearly 500,000 sales from the previous week. The sudden jump in sales was the largest ever documented barring irregular releases.

Accepting her sixth award at the Grammys in 2012 was emotional for Adele, who tied a record with that win.

would never sing again. Then she mouthed humble thank-yous to the crowd as they rose to their feet and bathed her in applause.

Adele mounted the stage twice more that evening. First, to collect her fifth award, for Record of the Year. But Adele's crowning achievement came at the end of the night when 21 was deemed Album of the Year. By winning six Grammy Awards, Adele tied a record with R&B singer Beyoncé for most awards won by a female singer in a single night. A tearful Adele slowly made her way to the stage, hugging people along the way. Adele was no less candid than usual during her acceptance speech. About halfway through, she confessed she was fighting a losing battle with the enemy of all Grammy Award winners: snot. After making a hilarious show of sniffing and wiping, she thanked her crew and loved ones.

BRIT AWARDS, *VOGUE*, AND CONTROVERSY

Less than two weeks after sweeping the Grammys, Adele was set for a repeat performance at the BRIT Awards in London. By the end of the night, she had claimed the award for British Female Solo Artist and wowed her hometown audience with another live rendition of "Rolling in the Deep." Finally, the presenter for British Album of the Year took the stage. No one was surprised when he announced Adele as the winner. The shock came when, just

Adele clutching her awards at
the BRIT Awards in 2012

as Adele was beginning her speech by expressing how proud she was to be British and to have won this award, the host of the show cut her off. Adele responded by flipping the bird to the producers of the show.

The spirited singer later apologized for making the gesture and made it clear it wasn't meant for her fans. It had been aimed at what Adele called the "suits" who decided to cut her speech short.[1] Adele's fans seemed as offended as she was that her big moment was spoiled. ITV, the network that broadcast the BRIT Awards, smoothed things over by issuing Adele an apology.

Adele's fans were also buzzing about the singer's image on the March 2012 cover of US *Vogue*. In the photo, her features seemed airbrushed to make her appear thinner. Those who looked up to Adele as a role model for average-sized women were disappointed with the fashion magazine for portraying her unrealistically. Regardless of the questionable photos, Adele's personality was faithfully—and charmingly—represented in the article that appeared in the magazine's interior. In the interview, Adele hinted at what lay ahead for her.

In search of a more private retreat from the media, Adele rented a sprawling mansion tucked away in the countryside of Surrey, England, in 2012. The ten-bedroom brick home sits on 25 acres (10 ha) and boasts two swimming pools, a tennis court, and a helicopter landing pad. The mansion, originally built for an aristocratic family, was worth more than £6 million (more than $9 million) when Adele took up residence there with Konecki in early 2012.

BEYOND 21

When asked how she envisioned her future, Adele told *Vogue*:

> *I am [taking a break] for four or five years. If I am constantly working, my relationships fail. So at least now I can have enough time to write a happy record. And be in love. . . . And then I don't know what I'll do. Get married. Have some kids. Plant a nice vegetable patch.*[2]

However, according to her blog, that four or five year break she mentioned would be condensed into just a few days. Then she promised to go straight to work on her next album. As for marriage, Adele's ring-finger bling at both the Grammys and the BRITs sparked rumors she was already engaged to Konecki. As of October 2012, these rumors had yet to be confirmed. Nonetheless, Adele was thrilled to announce some other good news on June 29, 2012. She announced she and Konecki were expecting a child. "Obviously we're over the moon and very excited," she said of her pregnancy.[3] On October 19, Adele and Konecki welcomed their son into the world.

At least for now, Adele doesn't plan to put her career on hold. The star premiered a new single on October 5. The song, "Skyfall," is the theme song for a movie of the same name, the 2012 installment of the James Bond series. Sources also reported in

21 TRIUMPHS

Adele's *21* achieved record-breaking success around the world. By May 2012, the album was certified platinum 16 times over in the United Kingdom, with sales of more than 4 million in the United Kingdom alone. That made it the album with the fifth-highest sales of all time in the United Kingdom. *21* topped the UK charts for an astounding 23 weeks, longer than any album has held the Number 1 spot in more than 40 years. In the United States, *21* was the best-selling album of 2011 and hovered at or near the top of the charts throughout the year. Worldwide, it was the best-selling album of the decade, with more than 18 million copies sold.

October that the singer was at work on her next album. As *US Weekly* reported, "The pregnancy has had a big impact on her songwriting!"[4]

Adele firmly believes she still has room to grow musically. "I won't come out with new music until it's better than *21*," she has said.[5] Whatever inspires Adele's next album, it is sure to display the profound talent of a singer-songwriter whose early success has outshone the lifetime achievements of countless musicians. And that album will surely be a hit.

||||||||||

Adele's future was full of possibility in 2012, with a new son and aspirations to continue growing musically.

TIMELINE

1988

Adele Laurie Blue Adkins is born on May 5 to Penny Adkins and Mark Evans.

1999

Eleven-year-old Adele's grandfather dies. Her father succumbs to alcoholism, and Adele breaks off contact with him.

2002

At 14, Adele enrolls in the BRIT School, where she is encouraged to follow her dream of becoming a professional singer.

2007

Adele finds out her boyfriend has cheated on her. Their breakup inspires her to write the rest of the songs for her debut album.

2007

Adele is announced as the first-ever winner of the Critic's Choice BRIT Award in December.

2008

In late January, Adele releases *19* in the United Kingdom.

2004

Adele's friend sets up a MySpace Web page and posts recordings of the first three songs Adele wrote: "Hometown Glory," "Daydreamer," and "My Same."

2006

Adele graduates from the BRIT School in May. Her MySpace demos have already attracted the attention of record labels.

2006

In September, Adele is signed to XL Recordings.

2008

Adele's tour An Evening with Adele begins in May.

2008

On June 10, Adele releases *19* in the United States.

2008

Adele performs on *Saturday Night Live* on October 18. Immediately afterward, the popularity of *19* skyrockets.

TIMELINE

2009

Adele attends her first Grammy Awards on February 8. She wins two awards and performs "Chasing Pavements."

2009

Adele breaks up with her current beau in the spring. Again inspired by heartbreak, she starts working on her next album.

2009

On June 28, Adele headlines a sold-out show at the Hollywood Bowl in Los Angeles after Etta James falls ill.

2011

Adele begins dating Simon Konecki in October.

2011

After cancelling several performances due to voice troubles, Adele has a severe vocal hemorrhage in October. She cancels the final leg of her Adele Live tour.

2011

On November 3, Adele undergoes surgery on her throat to repair her vocal cords.

2011

2011

2011

Adele releases her second album, *21*, on January 24 in Europe and February 22 in the United States.

Adele begins her concert tour Adele Live in March.

In September, Adele performs at Royal Albert Hall. The performance is filmed and later released on DVD.

2012

2012

2012

Adele performs for the first time since her surgery and takes home all six awards for which she was nominated at the Grammy Awards on February 12.

Adele's song "Skyfall," the theme for the James Bond movie of the same name, premieres on October 5.

Adele's son is born on October 19.

GET THE SCOOP

FULL NAME

Adele Laurie Blue Adkins

DATE OF BIRTH

May 5, 1988

PLACE OF BIRTH

Tottenham, North London,
United Kingdom

ALBUMS

19 (2008), *21* (2011)

SELECTED TOURS

An Evening with Adele (2008), Adele Live (2011)

SELECTED AWARDS

- Won the BRIT Awards Critic's Choice Award for *19* in 2008
- Won Best New Artist for *19* at the Grammy Awards in 2009
- Won Best Female Pop Vocal Performance for "Chasing Pavements" at the Grammy Awards in 2009
- Won Album of the Year for *21* at the Grammy Awards in 2012

- Won Best Pop Vocal Album for *21* at the Grammy Awards in 2012
- Won Record of the Year for "Rolling in the Deep" at the Grammy Awards in 2012
- Won Song of the Year for "Rolling in the Deep" at the Grammy Awards in 2012
- Won Best Short Form Music Video for "Rolling in the Deep" at the Grammy Awards in 2012
- Won Best Pop Solo Performance for "Someone Like You" at the Grammy Awards in 2012
- Won British Female Solo Artist of the Year for *21* at the BRIT Awards in 2012
- Won MasterCard British Album of the Year for *21* at the BRIT Awards in 2012

PHILANTHROPY

Adele has raised money for Sands, a UK charity devoted to research and prevention of infant death. In 2011, Adele mandated all tickets acquired for free for her Adele Live concert tour be matched by the recipient in the form of a minimum $20 donation to Sands. The donations raised for the charity amounted to $13,000.

"I don't make music for eyes. I make music for ears."

—ADELE

GLOSSARY

a cappella—Without the accompaniment of music.

acoustic—Relating to music in which sound is not enhanced by electronics.

alcoholism—A disease characterized by addiction to alcoholic beverages.

candid—Honest or sincere.

chart—A weekly listing of songs or albums in order of popularity or record sales.

collaborate—To work together in order to create or produce a work, such as a song or album.

debut—A first appearance.

demo—An initial recording meant to demonstrate a musician's talent to a record producer.

Grammy Award—One of several awards the National Academy of Recording Arts and Sciences presents each year to honor musical achievement.

hemorrhage—Extensive and uncontrolled bleeding.

hip-hop—A style of popular music associated with American urban culture that features rap spoken against a background of electronic music beats.

longevity—How long something lasts.

lyricism—Expression presented in a beautiful way in poetry or lyrics.

prestigious—Important or highly respected.

prodigy—An extraordinarily talented youth.

producer—Someone who oversees or provides money for a play, television show, movie, or album.

prophetic—Predictive of future events.

pyrotechnics—Fireworks and other special effects using explosions.

record label—A brand or trademark related to the marketing of music videos and recordings.

rhythm and blues —A kind of music that—especially in modern times—typically combines hip-hop, soul, and funk.

single—An individual song that is distributed on its own over the radio and other mediums.

studio—A room with electronic recording equipment where music is recorded.

track—A portion of a recording contract containing a single song or a piece of music.

venue—The place where a concert or other event is held.

ADDITIONAL RESOURCES

SELECTED BIBLIOGRAPHY

Bowles, Hamish. "Adele: Feeling Groovy." *Vogue*. Conde Nast, Apr. 2009. Web. 29 June 2012.

Newkey-Burden, Chas. *Adele: The Biography*. London: John Blake, 2011. Print.

Toure. "Adele Opens Up about Her Inspirations, Looks, and Stage Fright." *Rolling Stone*. Rolling Stone, 28 Apr. 2011. Web. 3 Aug. 2012.

Van Meter, Jonathan. "Adele: One and Only." *Vogue*. Conde Nast, 13 Feb. 2012. Web. 27 June 2012.

FURTHER READINGS

Shapiro, Marc. *Adele: The Biography*. New York: St. Martin's Griffin, 2012. Print.

Suhr, H. Cecilia. *Social Media and Music: The Digital Field of Cultural Production*. New York: Peter Lang, 2012. Print.

WEB SITES

To learn more about Adele, visit ABDO Publishing Company online at **www.abdopublishing.com**. Web sites about Adele are featured on our Book Links page. These links are routinely monitored and updated to provide the most current information available.

PLACES TO VISIT

The BRIT School
60 The Crescent, Croydon CR0 2HN, United Kingdom
0208-665-5242
www.brit.croydon.sch.uk
Visit the famous school that helped turn Adele, Amy Winehouse, Kate Nash, and others into star musicians.

Royal Albert Hall
Royal Albert Hall
Kensington Gore, London SW7 2 AP, United Kingdom
0845-401-5045
www.royalalberthall.com
Attend an event at or take a tour of the historic concert hall where Adele performed live just before cancelling the rest of her Adele Live tour.

SOURCE NOTES

CHAPTER 1. CHASING PAVEMENTS, CHASING DREAMS

1. Melinda Newman. "Amy Who? Now, Adele's the One with the Buzz." *Washington Post*. Washington Post, 1 Feb. 2009. Web. 25 June 2012.

2. Jon Bream. "Music: Chasing Adele." *StarTribune*. StarTribune, 15 Jan 2009. Web. 3 Aug. 2012.

3. "2009 GRAMMY Awards: Adele Wins Best New Artist." *YouTube*. YouTube, 11 Feb. 2009. Web. 3 Aug. 2012.

4. Ibid.

5. Georgie Rogers. "Adele 'Not Ready' to Win Grammy." *BBC News*. BBC, 5 Dec. 2008. Web. 25 June 2012.

6. "Adele: VH1 News Confidential at the 51st Annual Grammy Awards." *YouTube*. YouTube, 17 Mar. 2012. Web. 25 June 2012.

CHAPTER 2. ADELE LAURIE BLUE

1. Emily Hill. "Painful Past Behind Huge Hits for Adele." *Telegraph*. Telegraph Media Group, 10 July 2011. Web. 26 June 2012.

2. Chas Newkey-Burden. *Adele: The Biography*. London: John Blake, 2011. Print. 3.

3. "MTV Unplugged: Adele." *MTV*. Viacom International, 2012. Web. 26 June 2012.

4. Hamish Bowles. "Adele: Feeling Groovy." *Vogue*. Condé Nast, Apr. 2009. Web. 26 June 2012.

5. Ibid.

6. Stuart Husband. "Adele: Young Soul Rebel." *Telegraph*. Telegraph Media Group, 27 Apr. 2008. Web. 26 June 2012.

7. Simon Cable. "Adele Beats Lady Gaga to No. 1." *Mail Online*. Associated Newspapers, 21 Feb. 2011. Web. 26 June 2012.

8. Grant Rollings and Nic North. "'I Was an Alcoholic and Rotten Dad to Adele. It Tears Me Up Inside.'" *Sun*. News Group Newspapers, 16 Mar. 2011. Web. 26 June 2012.

9. Jonathan Van Meter. "Adele: One and Only." *Vogue*. Condé Nast, 13 Feb. 2012. Web. 26 June 2012.

CHAPTER 3. IMMERSED IN MUSIC

1. Hamish Bowles. "Adele: Feeling Groovy." *Vogue*. Condé Nast, Apr. 2009. Web. 27 June 2012.

2. "Shingai Shoniwa." *Glamour*. Condé Nast, 2012. Web. 27 June 2012.

CHAPTER 4. *19*

1. Hamish Bowles. "Adele: Feeling Groovy." *Vogue*. Condé Nast, Apr. 2009. Web. 27 June 2012.

2. Jonathan Van Meter. "Adele: One and Only." *Vogue*. Condé Nast, 13 Feb. 2012. Web. 27 June 2012.

3. Caspar Llewellyn Smith. "Adele, 19." *Guardian*. Guardian News and Media, 19 Jan. 2008. Web. 3 Aug. 2012.

4. Ibid.

CHAPTER 5. ADELE IN AMERICA

1. Toure. "Adele Opens Up about Her Inspirations, Looks, and Stage Fright." *Rolling Stone*. Rolling Stone, 28 Apr. 2011. Web. 3 Aug. 2012.

2. "Adele North American Tour 2008." *YouTube*. YouTube, 17 Mar. 2011. Web. 28 June 2012.

3. "Adele." *Billboard*. Billboard, 7 June 2008. *Google Book Search*. Web. 3 Aug. 2012.

4. Hamish Bowles. "Adele: Feeling Groovy." *Vogue*. Condé Nast, Apr. 2009. Web. 28 June 2012.

5. "Adele Explains 2008 Booze & Love Meltdown." *Contactmusic. com*. Contactmusic.com, 8 June 2009. Web. 28 June 2012.

6. Ibid.

7. Jonathan Van Meter. "Adele: One and Only." *Vogue*. Condé Nast, 13 Feb. 2012. Web. 28 June 2012.

CHAPTER 6. *21*

1. "Adele on Q TV." *YouTube*. YouTube, 29 June 2009. Web. 29 June 2012.

2. Adrian Thrills. "'I'm a Failure . . . That's Why I Sing': Never Mind the Hits, Adele Reveals that She Is Fueled by Pain and Insecurity." *Mail Online*. Associated Newspapers, 20 Jan. 2011. Web. 29 June 2012.

SOURCE NOTES CONTINUED

3. Hamish Bowles. "Adele: Feeling Groovy." *Vogue*. Condé Nast, Apr. 2009. Web. 29 June 2012.

4. Zach Johnson. "Adele: I Don't Want to Be Some Skinny Mini." *US Weekly*. Wenner Media, 2012. 9 Feb. 2012. Web. 3 Aug. 2012.

5. Adele Adkins. "So Much." *Adele*. Adele, 15 May 2009. *Bebo*. Web. 29 June 2012.

6. Alison Boshoff and Sara Nathan. "'I Just Want to Say, Mum . . . Your Girl Did Good!' Adele's Touching Tribute as She Scoops Six Grammys." *Mail Online*. Associated Newspapers, 14 Feb. 2012. Web. 29 June 2012.

7. James C. McKinley Jr. "Hot Tracks, the Collaborative Method." *New York Times*. New York Times, 9 Feb. 2012. Web. 29 June 2012.

8. "The Adele Experience." *PRS for Music Online Magazine*. PRS for Music, 22 Dec. 2011. Web. 29 June 2012.

CHAPTER 7. ADELE LIVE

1. Ian Wade. "Adele 21 Review." *BBC Music*. BBC, 17 Jan. 2011. Web. 29 June 2012.

2. Will Dean. "Adele: 21 Review." *Guardian*. Guardian News and Media, 20 Jan 2011. Web. 29 June 2012.

3. Robin Murray. "Adele Talks BRIT Award Performance." *Clash Music*. Clash Music, 17 Feb. 2011. Web. 29 June 2012.

4. Jonathan Van Meter. "Adele: One and Only." *Vogue*. Condé Nast, 13 Feb. 2012. Web. 29 June 2012.

CHAPTER 8. RIGHT AS RAIN

1. "Adele Flips Off Producers at BRIT Awards." *CBS News*. CBS Interactive, 22 Feb. 2012. Web. 1 July 2012.

2. Jonathan Van Meter. "Adele: One and Only." *Vogue*. Condé Nast, 13 Feb. 2012. Web. 1 July 2012.

3. Adele Adkins. "I've Got Some News . . ." *Adele*. Adele, 29 June 2012. Web. 2 July 2012.

4. "Adele Gives Birth to Baby Boy!" *US Weekly*. US Weekly, 21 Oct. 2012. Web. 22 Oct. 2012.

5. Jonathan Van Meter. "Adele: One and Only." *Vogue*. Condé Nast, 13 Feb. 2012. Web. 1 July 2012.

INDEX

ABOUT THE AUTHOR

Lisa Owings has a degree in English and creative writing from the University of Minnesota. She has written and edited a wide variety of educational books for young people. Lisa lives in Andover, Minnesota, with her husband and a small menagerie of pets.

PHOTO CREDITS